Please visit our website, www.enslow.com. For a free color catalog of all our high-quality books, call toll free 1-800-398-2504 or fax 1-877-980-4454.

Library of Congress Cataloging-in-Publication Data

Names: Tobler, Elise, 1970– author.
Title: Chameleons change color! / Elise Tobler.
Description: New York : Enslow Publishing, [2021] | Series: Reptiles rock!
   | Includes index.
Identifiers: LCCN 2019051692 | ISBN 9781978518148 (library binding) | ISBN
   9781978518124 (paperback) | ISBN 9781978518131 (six pack) | ISBN 9781978518155
   (ebook)
Subjects: LCSH: Chameleons—Color—Juvenile literature. |
   Chameleons—Behavior—Juvenile literature.
Classification: LCC QL666.L23 T63 2021 | DDC 597.95/6—dc23
LC record available at https://lccn.loc.gov/2019051692

Published in 2021 by
Enslow Publishing
101 West 23rd Street, Suite #240
New York, NY 10011

Copyright © 2021 Enslow Publishing

Designer: Laura Bowen
Editor: Elise Tobler

Photo credits: Cover, p. 1 (chameleon) PetlinDmitry/Shutterstock.com; cover, pp. 1–32 (leaves border) Marina Solva/Shutterstock.com; p. 5 Kuttelvaserova Stuchelova/Shutterstock.com; p. 7 (map) zeber/Shutterstock.com; p. 7 (Madagascar) Vaclav Sebek/Shutterstock.com; p. 9 Irina Kozorog/Shutterstock.com; pp. 10, 11 (bottom) Cathy Keifer/Shutterstock.com; p. 11 (top) Luke Wait/Shutterstock.com; p. 12 Chantelle Bosch/Shutterstock.com; pp. 13, 21 (right) Eric Isselee/Shutterstock.com; p. 14 Jan Bures/Shutterstock.com; p. 15 (left) MyImages - Micha/Shutterstock.com; p. 15 (right) GlobalP/iStock.com; p. 17 Ferdy Timmerman/Shutterstock.com; p. 18 xlt974/Shutterstock.com; p. 19 Baishev/Shutterstock.com; p. 21 (left) Dewald Kirsten/Shutterstock.com; p. 22 Daniel Mietchen/Wikimedia Commons; p. 23 (both) Nick Henn/Shutterstock.com; p. 24 larus/Shutterstock.com; p. 25 Suren Tsormudyan/Shutterstock.com; p. 27 Daniel Barquero/Shutterstock.com; p. 29 (main) Hugh Lansdown/Shutterstock.com; p. 29 (inset) Neel Adsul/Shutterstock.com.

Portions of this work were originally authored by Kathleen Connors and published as *Chameleons*. All new material in this edition authored by Elise Tobler.

All rights reserved. No part of this book may be reproduced in any form without permission in writing from the publisher, except by a reviewer.

Printed in the United States of America

Some of the images in this book illustrate individuals who are models. The depictions do not imply actual situations or events.

CPSIA compliance information: Batch #BS20ENS: For further information contact Enslow Publishing, New York, New York, at 1-800-398-2504.

CONTENTS

Ground Lion 4
Right at Home 6
A Well-Balanced Diet 8
A Talented Tongue 10
Super Vision 12
A Curly Tail 14
Happy Feet 16
Masters of Disguise 18
Family Time 20
Baby Chameleons 22
An Old Species 24
Chameleons as Pets 26
Future Chameleons 28
Glossary 30
For More Information 31
Index 32

Words in the glossary appear in **bold** type the first time they are used in the text.

GROUND LION

The word "chameleon" means "ground lion" in Greek, which may seem strange since chameleons usually live in trees. You may see that they do look like lions, with their long tail, claws, and head crest. Chameleons look more fierce than they are.

There are more than 200 different kinds of chameleons throughout the world, and scientists are still discovering new ones. Chameleons are known for the ways their eyes can move, fast tongues, and color-changing abilities. Chameleons can be as small as 1 inch (2.5 cm) in length, but many grow bigger.

RIGHT AT HOME

Almost half of the world's chameleon population lives on the island of Madagascar, off the east coast of Africa. Chameleons live in rain forests, deserts, and **steppes**. Chameleons are usually arboreal—meaning they live in trees or bushes—but you can also find them on the ground or among rocks.

GET THE FACTS!

You can find chameleons in places like Hawaii and Florida, but only because those chameleons were kept as pets and escaped or were released by their owners. If you have a pet chameleon, never let it loose outside.

Many species of chameleon are in danger of dying out. The threat to chameleons comes largely from **habitat** loss. Rain forests are at risk because of climate change, or the slow warming of Earth, and the clearing of land for cattle to feed.

Chameleons prefer warm places like Africa and Madagascar.

AFRICA

Madagascar

Madagascar

A WELL-BALANCED DIET

Unlike you, chameleons can't just go into the kitchen when they're hungry. They have to track their food down in the wild. Wild chameleons like to eat crickets, worms, cockroaches, and flies. They also eat grasshoppers.

If a chameleon is being kept as a pet, its diet might be different, consisting of green leafy vegetables such as collard greens and mustard greens. You can also buy crickets and other small insects at pet stores to feed your chameleon for variety.

GET THE FACTS!

Someone who studies reptiles and **amphibians** is called a herpetologist. Amphibians include frogs, salamanders, and newts, and they need a wet environment to live. Reptiles, like chameleons, can live in dry deserts or wet rain forests.

Chameleons' favorite foods are usually bugs.

A TALENTED TONGUE

A chameleon's tongue can be 1.5 times as long as its body. If your tongue was like a chameleon tongue, your tongue would be 6 to 8 feet (1.8 to 2.4 m) long! Like a bow and arrow, a chameleon pulls back on its tongue and shoots its tongue from its mouth to catch food.

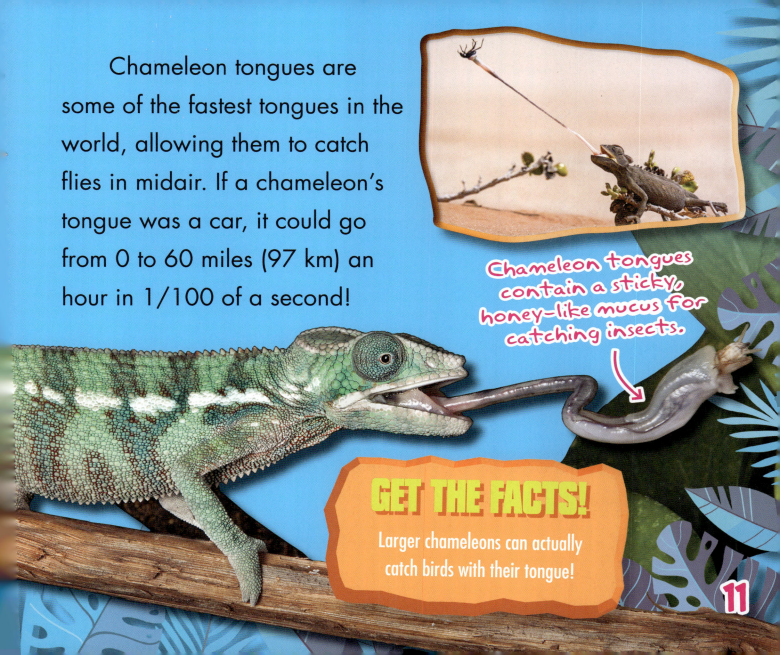

Chameleon tongues are some of the fastest tongues in the world, allowing them to catch flies in midair. If a chameleon's tongue was a car, it could go from 0 to 60 miles (97 km) an hour in 1/100 of a second!

Chameleon tongues contain a sticky, honey-like mucus for catching insects.

GET THE FACTS!

Larger chameleons can actually catch birds with their tongue!

SUPER VISION

Chameleon eyes aren't like human eyes. Each eye can move independently and can look almost 360° around. Chameleons can look at something with both eyes or with only one eye. You would have to close one eye to do that!

This helps chameleons find more food because they can look in more than one place at once. It also helps them avoid predators because they can see danger approaching from all sides. This improves their **reflexes**, allowing them to escape danger when other reptiles might be caught.

Each chameleon eye moves independently of the other one.

GET THE FACTS!

As good as a chameleon's eyes are, its hearing isn't that great. Chameleons can hear only a limited range of sounds. They don't have an outer ear, only a little earhole near their eyes.

A CURLY TAIL

A chameleon tail is prehensile, which means chameleons can grasp things with it. They can curl their tail around tree branches to hold on, just like you might with a hand. The tail allows them to be more flexible.

Their tail also allows them to hold on when they shoot their tongue at prey. When a chameleon rests,

GET THE FACTS!

Are you thinking about getting a chameleon for a pet? Be sure you know its length measurement from its nose to the tip of its tail so you can get a tank that is large enough for it to be comfortable.

it curls its tail up close to its body. Some lizards have tails that will regrow if the tail is cut off or shed, but a chameleon tail will not regrow.

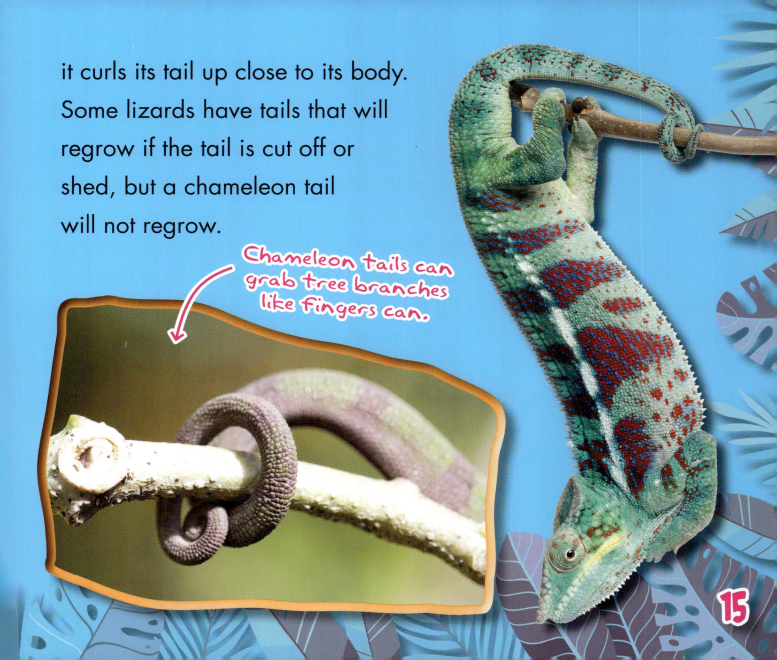

Chameleon tails can grab tree branches like fingers can.

HAPPY FEET

Chameleon feet are some of the fanciest in the animal kingdom. Chameleons have two outer toes and three inner toes, which help them stay on branches when they are climbing, sleeping, or hunting for food. Each toe has a sharp nail that can help them climb by digging into the tree bark.

Other animals, like sloths, have similar feet, but only chameleons have toes that form in groups to help them climb. Chameleon feet are not sticky like gecko feet. Chameleons rely on their grip and their sharp nails to keep them on tree branches. Their curling tail also helps them.

Chameleons are some of the best climbers in the world.

GET THE FACTS!

Chameleon feet and toes are similar to human hands. Their toes act the way our thumb does with our fingers, allowing them to grasp branches and other things of interest. These kind of feet are often called zygodactyl (zy-goh-DAK-tuhl).

MASTERS OF DISGUISE

Most chameleons can change their color. It was once thought that this was to hide. So, for example, if a chameleon was in a tree, it could be green to match the leaves. On the ground, a chameleon might be brown to hide in the dirt.

We now know that chameleons can change color in response to how hot or cold it is, the time of the day, or even their mood. If a chameleon is cold, it increases the number of dark-colored **pigments** in its scales. This helps it stay warm because darker colors take in more heat from the sun.

The scales on a chameleon allow it to change colors.

GET THE FACTS!
Scientists used to think that chameleons changed color only to hide, but now they believe the color change is also a way to communicate with other chameleons.

FAMILY TIME

Chameleons prefer to live alone. When male chameleons are put in a cage together, they will fight each other rather than live in peace. Chameleons usually come together only when it's time to mate, or try and produce babies, which can happen up to three times a year.

Male chameleons will change colors as a way of asking female chameleons if they are ready to mate.

GET THE FACTS!

Male chameleons often have brighter colors than female chameleons. Males can also be larger, have bigger crests, and have spurs on their back legs. Male chameleons will also often have horns, which females do not have.

Female chameleons can change colors to show that they are ready or not, and they may also hiss at males if the males are too determined.

Male chameleons often have horns. Females do not.

BABY CHAMELEONS

Females of some chameleon species will give birth to anywhere from 8 to 30 live babies at a time after carrying them for 4 to 6 months. Many other chameleons will lay eggs, which can take 4 to 24 months to hatch, which means the babies come out of their shell.

GET THE FACTS!

The entire process of hatching from an egg can take up to a day, with the baby chameleon using its egg tooth to break the shell open. Some chameleons are only as big as a dime when they are born!

Like chickens, not all chameleon eggs have babies in them. These eggs, just like those in your refrigerator, will not hatch. In the wild, chameleons will often lay their eggs in sand or dirt. The babies have to crawl up and out when they hatch.

Some chameleons are born live, while others hatch from eggs.

AN OLD SPECIES

There are more than 200 kinds of chameleons in the world. Chameleons have been around a lot longer than humans have. Chameleons as we know them probably weren't alive during the time of the dinosaurs, but their ancestors were. Many lizards have been found **preserved** in tree sap (amber).

One of these preserved lizards had the same kind of tongue we see in chameleons today, but it had not yet developed the fancy feet for gripping. Ancient forests would have been a great place for chameleons to live. This reinforces why we should care for rain forests today.

GET THE FACTS!

The geckos, lizards, and chameleons that have been found in amber were tiny—some as small as a dime—so their preservation is an incredible look at a world we wouldn't otherwise know. The amber helped save them for us to study.

Lizards and chameleons have been found preserved in tree sap.

CHAMELEONS AS PETS

Chameleons, like other lizards, are often kept as pets. But chameleons have certain needs to keep them happy, even though you don't have to walk them like a dog. Chameleons like being alone, so don't keep more than one in a tank at a time.

You may need to get a heating lamp to ensure the chameleon is never too cold.

You should be prepared to feed them their favorite food: bugs! Your local pet store can tell you more about keeping chameleons as pets.

GET THE FACTS!

When getting a pet chameleon, you'll want to find one that was bred in **captivity**. Wild chameleons are often highly unhappy when confined to a tank after roaming the wild forests. A happy pet chameleon is normally brightly colored.

You can't cuddle chameleons, but they're still fascinating!

FUTURE CHAMELEONS

We have learned about chameleons and lizards from millions of years ago because they were preserved in amber. Does this mean chameleons will be around a million years from now? They will be if we humans take good care of them! Preserving their homes in the rain forests is an important step.

Scientists have recently learned how to make an artificial, or man-made, chameleon skin. They can change the color of the material by changing its temperature. This might allow people of the future to wear chameleon-like clothes that change color with the weather!

GET THE FACTS!

Around 50 percent of the world's chameleon species live on the island of Madagascar. There are 59 species on Madagascar that live nowhere else in the world, so keeping the forests of the island safe and whole is important for chameleons.

Keeping the rain forests safe will help keep chameleons safe.

GLOSSARY

amphibian An animal that spends time on land but must have babies and grow into an adult in water.

captivity The state of being caged.

habitat The place or type of place where a plant or animal naturally or normally lives or grows.

lizard A type of reptile that has four legs and a long body and tail.

mucus A thick liquid that is produced in some parts of the body.

pigment A substance that gives a plant or animal color.

preserve To keep in good condition over a long period of time.

reflex An action or movement of the body that happens automatically as a reaction to something.

reptile An animal covered with scales or plates that breathes air, has a backbone, and lays eggs, such as a turtle, snake, lizard, or crocodile.

steppe A large, flat area of land with grass and very few trees.

FOR MORE INFORMATION

Books

Bodden, Valerie. *Chameleons.* Mankato, MN: Creative Paperbacks, 2016.

Kenan, Tessa. *It's a Chameleon!* Minneapolis, MN: Bumba Books, Lerner, 2017.

Quarry, Rachel. *Colin the Chameleon.* Adelaide, Australia: Starfish Bay Publishing, 2018.

Websites

Chameleon Facts for Kids
www.coolkidfacts.com/chameleon-facts-for-kids/
Amazing facts about chameleons, including "believe it or not" information.

Easy Science for Kids
easyscienceforkids.com/all-about-chameleons/
Learn more about how chameleons change their color.

National Geographic Kids: Chameleons
kids.nationalgeographic.com/animals/reptiles/chameleon/
A one-stop site for chameleon facts and slideshows.

Publisher's note to educators and parents: Our editors have carefully reviewed these websites to ensure that they are suitable for students. Many websites change frequently, however, and we cannot guarantee that a site's future contents will continue to meet our high standards of quality and educational value. Be advised that students should be closely supervised whenever they access the internet.

INDEX

amber/tree sap, 24, 25, 28

amphibians, 9

babies, 20, 22, 23

claws/nails, 4, 16

color/changing color, 4, 18, 19, 20, 21, 27

crests, 4, 20

diet, 8, 27

eyes, 4, 12, 13

feet, 16, 17, 25

habitat, 6, 7, 9

hearing, 13

lizards, 5, 15, 24, 25, 26, 28

mating, 20, 21

pet chameleons, 6, 8, 14, 26, 27

reptiles, 5, 9, 12

size, 4

tails, 4, 14, 15, 16

toes, 16, 17

tongues, 4, 10, 11, 14, 25